The Seasons of Advent

*A personal contemplation
By Susan Craig*

Gotham Books

30 N Gould St.
Ste. 20820, Sheridan, WY 82801
https://gothambooksinc.com/

Phone: 1 (307) 464-7800

© 2023 *Susan Craig*. All rights reserved.

No part of this book may be reproduced, stored in a retrieval system, or transmitted by any means without the written permission of the author.

Published by Gotham Books (September 9, 2023)

ISBN: 979-8-88775-408-6 (P)
ISBN: 979-8-88775-409-3 (E)

Because of the dynamic nature of the Internet, any web addresses or links contained in this book may have changed since publication and may no longer be valid.

The views expressed in this work are solely those of the author and do not necessarily reflect the views of the publisher, and the publisher hereby disclaims any responsibility for them.

My Journey to Faith

While it might not be the usual route taken to faith by many, my journey started within a family that had eschewed religious expression and avoided church going as a rule. This was a consequence of some unhappy encounters with the rules and regulations that man had yet again overlaid on the worship of God over time. However, there was something that piqued my curiosity and interest enough for me to investigate on my own. I wished to explore how the world came to be and what informed the order that was evident throughout nature. This curiosity combined with a scientific background, and the loves for both reading and history, set me on a journey of questioning and searching. From the time I was high school age onward I explored as many avenues as I possibly could to explain patterns and the origins. When I could no longer argue that there was not an overarching intelligence at work in the universe, I started looking into the various expressions of belief. That took up about thirty years of exploration. During this time, I looked at the many different expressions of acknowledging this intelligence behind the order of the universe. I explored many options atheist, agnostic, animist, and differing theistic belief systems. I was looking for consistency through the ages. I even looked at the possibility that this intelligence could and would communicate with His creation in whatever means that individual or group could best fathom. Yet over time I could no longer deny that the God who created us and loved us wanted to restore the communion and companionship of His creation that stood at Creation. Then He would provide an avenue for that to be accomplished for all who wished and chose to take that route. As none of us seem capable of achieving the perfection required through our own efforts and that only the "perfected" would be able to withstand his holy presence, then a safety measure is required. A covering much like a spacesuit, if you will, is needed for us to be able to stand in His presence and not be utterly destroyed. Well, in His time, He provided this covering for all who desire and seek to fill the hole that is left when a loved one is not available, as all creation desires a return to its original state of perfection. The season of Advent speaks of that longing. While it might not be the 'actual' season it is our commemoration of the fact that this return has been made possible by the advent of Jesus. Now I can echo the psalmist and have taken as my life verse Psalm 42:8.

> "By day the Lord directs his love,
> at night his song is with me —
> a prayer to the God of my life."
> Psalms 42: 8

Acknowledgements

There are several people without whom this book would never have come to be. I would be very remiss if I did not express my gratitude for their encouragement and assistance. I will attempt to express the depth of my appreciation and love I have for their assistance.

First off there is Pastor Mike Morrison whose challenges and encouragement helped me to overcome my hesitations about creative writing and sharing my efforts with others. He has stretched my abilities and his criticisms have been very constructive.

I'd like to thank the pastoral staff of my home church, Stanwood Community, who patiently endured my questions about Biblical texts. Graciously and generously giving of their time. Without this help I would have hesitated to put forward this book.

A very gracious and good friend who consented to review my manuscript prior to submission and gave me some good pointers. Thank you very much, C. J. Lewis, for you confidence and encouragement.

Lastly and most importantly, God who has encouraged my curiosity to study and to investigate His Word and loving kindnesses. He has lead me to portions of His living word that had previously been confusing and illuminated them with a new understanding.

Without these, this effort would not have come to be and my understanding of Advent would not have taken on a new richness and depth.

So with gratitude I acknowledge and thank all who by their love and support (both great and small) have encouraged me to continue in this effort which I admit I entered into with great trepidations.

Contents

As I was writing these essays, there were songs and sounds that were running through my mind as an accompaniment to the thoughts I was trying to express. The list is given here just for your enjoyment or use while reading or discussing.

I.	Introduction: Advent Seasons	pg. 1
II.	A Season of Hope	pg. 4
	Essay 1. Anticipation	pg. 6
	The Hymn - Soon and very Soon	
	Essay 2. Expectation	pg. 8
	The Hymn - Come thou font of Every Blessing	
	Essay 3. Preparation	pg. 11
	Song by the HiLo's - Something's Coming	
	The Hymn - Prepare ye the way of the Lord	
	Essay 4. Transformation	pg. 13
	The Hymn - Create in me a Clean Heart	
III.	A Season of Gladness	pg. 18
	Essay 1. Illumination	pg. 19
	The Hymn - Light of the World, You stepped down into darkness	
	Essay 2. Celebration	pg. 22
	Gaither Homecoming song - Rejoice with exceeding great joy	
	Essay 3. Appreciation	pg. 24
	The Hymn - And Can It Be	
	Essay 4. Jubilation	pg. 26
	Sounding of the Shofar	
	Paul Wilbur Song - Shouts of Joy	
IV.	A Season of Promise	pg. 30
	Essay 1. Constant	pg. 31
	The Hymn - O God, Our Help in Ages Past	
	Essay 2. Guidance	pg. 34
	The Hymn - The Lord is my Shepherd	
	Essay 3. Providence	pg. 37
	Andrew Peterson song - Labor of Love (Behold the Lamb)	
	Essay 4. Comfort	pg. 40
	From The Comforting Hand of God - Beholding the Awesome Glory of God!	

V.	A Season of Love	pg. 43
	Essay 1. Persevering	pg. 45
	The Song - I'll Walk with God	
	Essay 2. Faithful	pg. 47
	The Hymn - Great is Thy Faithfulness	
	Essay 3. Forgiving	pg. 50
	The Hymn - In Tenderness, He Sought Me	
	Essay 4. True	pg. 52
	The Hymn - Immortal, Invisible God Only Wise	
VI.	Summary: The Wonder of Advent	pg. 56
	The Hymn - I Wonder as I Wander	
VII.	Conclusion - The Reason for the Advent	pg. 59
	The Hymns - Amazing Grace	
	- Amazing Love	
	Essay 1. Manumission	pg. 62
	Essay 2. Reconciliation	pg. 66
	Essay 3. Restoration	pg. 72
Footnotes:		pg. 75

*Unless notated all Biblical quotes are from the New International Translation (NIV)

Advent Seasons

For a long time, we have referred to the season leading up to Christmas as Advent. But what is an advent. First an advent is an arrival or a coming into being, so this season is a commemoration of the arrival of Christ to reside with us. It has the connotation of a dawning or the start of something momentous. However, as I studied what this advent meant to me, I came to see it as having four different characteristics or seasons, if you will, that spoke to me. These characteristics were epitomized by the elements of hope, gladness, promise, and love. Two are our proper responses to two of the characteristics of who God is and what He has done for us. Our responses of hope and gladness are founded in now seeing and commemorating a proof positive that God truly does concern Himself with us and we no longer have to wish that we had means of returning to His presence without fear. The portions of God's character that were most on display during Advent were His love for mankind and His fulfillment of promise.

A Season of Hope: Hope speaks of our longing for a closeness with God our Creator including the emotions of anticipation and expectation. Hope is an expression of our confidence in the fulfillment of God's promises. Lastly, it asks of us to make preparation and, ultimately, to undergo a transformation within our hearts.

A Season of <u>Gladness</u>: This describes our response to the proof that God is in control and does indeed love us beyond measure. This all-encompassing gladness starts with the lightness that enters into our lives when we recognize God's great love for us. Then it speaks of a growing thankfulness as well as the celebration and jubilation that fills our hearts as we see God's promises come to life.

A Season of <u>Promise</u>: Because in the evidence of the pronouncements that God has made and those that have come to fruition we can rest in confidence and faith that those not yet accomplished will also come into being. With the Advent of Christ, we are given proof of the greatest of his promises: that He continues to care for us. He has promised to be a steady and constant guiding hand in our lives, has promised to provide for us, and to comfort us as we abide in his Word.

A Season of <u>Love</u>: In the New Testament we are given a description of what ideal love looks like in 1 Corinthians chapter 13. From the beginning God has demonstrated this love. With the Advent of Christ, His love was given human form, and became approachable. The four elements of love that Advent brought to mind when considering God's love as expressed in Advent; were God's perseverance, faithfulness, His eagerness to forgive us, and the truth that is found in Him.

Then within each "season" I chose four components that go into that "season's title" that spoke most to my heart about the Advent of Christ. So, we may joyously celebrate as we consider the love that brought Christ into the world. This look into what Advent meant to me caused me to rethink how I viewed this annual commemoration. No longer was it merely the birth and coming hope but I came to see the cost and deep desire that underlay the event as well. I hope it does the same for you.

As this study was coming to an end there was a growing sense that it would be good to continue further. I was then inexorably drawn to continuing study to investigate what the reasons underlying God's magnanimous gift. Why was it necessary for the anticipated Messiah to come in a manner so totally unexpected? How was this plan of salvation to unfold? Then, what had He told us to prepare us for this gift? While everyone was looking for a political and military Savior who would bring Israel out of subjugation to Rome, God gave us His perfect Lamb. Therefore, I understood that God's purpose was not political it was to be healing and inclusive. In the end Jesus came as our Guardian-Redeemer to start our return to a right standing with God to what it had been in Eden. I discuss what I found in the sections "The Wonder of Advent" and "The Reasons for the Advent".

I saw that much of the wonder came from the evidence that when God entered into this world it was with awareness of the extreme cost that would be incurred for the purpose bringing mankind back to Him.

I found three main portions of the plan that were implemented during Advent. These set the conditions that are necessary to the end of repairing the relationship between God and all of Creation. These covered the providing the freedom from the bondage of sin that disrupted our companionship. The next element that in the process would be a reconciliation. A reconciliation that satisfies the debts and grievances that have been incurred. Then last would come a complete restoration. Advent provides, a surety for the promise that this restoration will be consummated in the future.

A Season of Hope

The word *hope* brings to mind a desire, a longing, or a want. It can also be something that is thought to be true, and for those that hold with this truth, the belief that it will happen. It holds a very real sense of anticipation as well as a set of expectations, and it indicates a need for some preparations in anticipation of that outcome. It involves our longings and our trust. It is when we have this hope that something is true; it causes a transformation in our outlook. The season of Advent is not only a commemoration of a time when that hope was answered, but it also encompasses the hope of one promised to us in the future.

This hope also contains a sense of trust and reliance on something or someone that engenders optimism for the future. This hope, when it is properly placed in God, who has and continues to provide help for a struggling and longing humanity, will strengthen our resolve. It is expressed in our desire, accompanied by the expectation and belief in fulfillment. It can and does encourage our preparation for the event as well as the transformation that occurs as our hope grows stronger.

Lastly, when our hope is centered on the Son of God, who was promised to come, came, and has promised to come again, we develop greater endurance. We can say the following, along with the psalmist:

> "Guard my life and rescue me; do not let
> me be put to shame, for I take refuge in
> you. May integrity and uprightness protect
> me, because my hope, Lord, is in you."
> — Psalm 25:20–21

This same Lord, our Christ, whose Advent we celebrate, is our guarantor, our friend, and our strength.

Essay: Anticipation

What would you feel like if you knew that very soon, you would have the opportunity to accept the offer of a complete amnesty for all your mistakes and debts, even the inadvertent ones made out of ignorance? This would create an eagerly awaited point in time. It would offer an eagerly anticipated sense of incredible release from all doubts and fears. This would be a jubilant event because it is a fantastic opportunity for expressions of joy and freedom. In each convicted heart a growing sense of anticipation would be building with every one of us eagerly looking to the day when we would be given the blessing of a clean slate. From the beginning it was understood that God was merciful, forgiving and just. It was what we expected at His hand by way of justice that worried us, we knew deeply what we were deserving of but the coming of Christ gives us the access to mercy and grace beyond payment. As it has been stated He is a one:

> "Who keeps mercy for thousands, who forgives iniquity, transgression and sin; yet He will by no means leave the guilty unpunished."
> —Exodus 34:7

In anticipation of that day, what would you deem necessary to accomplish so as to be prepared for that coming event? How would you ensure that you were rightly positioned and ready to receive this gift? What if you knew that you had nothing you could offer in return for this blessing and nothing could ever be of equivalent value to pay for it? Amazingly the giver of this great gift has declared that no reciprocation was required or even asked for!

> "See, I am sending an angel ahead of you to guard you along the way and to bring you to the place I have prepared."
> —Exodus 23:20

Wouldn't you be keeping an anxious watch to welcome the expected guide or would you be partying like there was nothing to worry about? Would you rush around gathering for yourself and others material things and worldly acclaim, or would you seek to bring this expectant joy to those around you? Would you keep the news to yourself? Most of us, I think, would be excitedly telling those around us of the long-awaited event so that they, too, might share in the excitement and joy!

> "Go to the great city of Nineveh and
> proclaim to it the message I give you."
> —Jonah 3: 2

So as the excitement builds to the awaited event it would be too much to hold inside. It would bubble up from deep within and burst out into our lives as expressions of great joy that would be impossible to contain. Nor are we supposed to suppress this response.

Essay: Expectation

We live with expectations every day. Often by the time we reach the conclusion, we find that many of these events, our expectations, came about in totally unexpected ways. For those of faith, we have all of the God-given promises which each of us expect to be fulfilled. While we often think that we know how these promises will be fulfilled, God continues to surprise us. Quite frequently we find that our expectations are confounded by God. Not only does He do things in His time, He does them in His own way, then many times to ends we do not foresee. This results in those faithfully keeping watch being surprised and sometimes disbelieving when the resolution presents itself.

> "For I know the plans I have for you,
> declares the Lord, plans for welfare and
> not for evil, to give you a future and a
> hope."
> —Jeremiah 29:11

Expectation: when we consider the how we use this word; we find that there are two meanings that are in use. One usage is built around our hopes and confidence in a promised event. The other usage is comprised of our assumptions of how our expectations are going to come to fruition.

We say we expect things to get better or to be shown a way out. The basis for the hope is past experience and our faith that the situation will change for the better. This hope expresses our confidence that God has concern for us and will provide.

We expect or think that these or those sorts of conditions or characteristics will be present in order for the improvement to occur. These are things that our senses of logic, tradition, and fairness would seem to tell us will be the proper means and methods. Regularly our understanding trips us up. Many times these assumptions are based on an incomplete or faulty understanding of the intent, purposes, and methods of God and cause us to look in the wrong directions for our coming salvation.

These assumptions, on many occasions has led us to be looking in all the wrong directions when our hoped-for solutions have arrived. Perhaps we should remember the frequent times in the past when God provided the promised event, but when it came, it came in manners, times, and places that were outside of the understanding and conventions of the time and society.

Here are four of the many times God has confounded the expectations of His people while perfectly providing the resolution of their hopes and expectations.

Case History I: A family of well-to-do people had the usual family tensions and petty jealousies; they finally got rid of the spoiled brat in their midst. A few years down the road they fell on some very serious hard times. Do you think they were looking to find their salvation in the one they had kicked out? [The story of Joseph]

Case History II: A tribal group who had moved into another land had been gradually taken advantage of, to the point of being under the total control of the native people. Do you think that they expected their deliverer to come in the form of one who had been raised in the lap of luxury, committed murder, and had fled to avoid the consequences of his actions? Do you think that they looked for a deliverer to be one uncomfortable speaking to crowds? Do you think they expected their rescuer to be one who had then lived as a shepherd, returning with only a staff as a weapon?

[The story of Moses]

Case History III: A fledgling nation has come under attack, and the people were desperately looking for a leader who could defeat the invading nation, which was vastly more powerful and better armed than they were. Not many would have thought that this great leader would come in the form of an unsure youth from the smallest and weakest of the tribes. Within that tribe his family was insignificant. Not only did God lead this young man against the invader but also against the vast numbers. Who would have thought God would have him attack with only three hundred men?

[The story of Gideon]

Case History IV: A conquered nation that is looking to throw off its conqueror was definitely not looking for their leader to come in the form of a teacher, especially a teacher who espoused love, kindness, forgiveness, and tolerance. Nor were they looking for one who would cause an upheaval in their religious practices. [The advent and story of Jesus]

Now in our times we, too, look for succor, and we have every reason and expectation that it will come about! However, what if we are looking in the wrong direction because our ways and thoughts are not God's? God in His wisdom has provided the solutions, but rarely has He done this in the manner expected by us. As He has declared:

> "For my thoughts are not your thoughts,
> neither are your ways my ways, declares
> the Lord. As the heavens are higher than
> the earth, so are my ways higher than your
> ways and my thoughts than your
> thoughts."
> —Isaiah 55: 8, 9

Essay: Preparation

You know something great is coming! The anticipation and expectations are building. The how and the when are as yet unknown, but yet you can feel the energy building, and you cannot keep it to yourself, nor are you supposed to! Just like the heralds of the past; who were sent out to announce the coming of the king, so should we herald our King's coming. To put it another way, we could serve like the advance men of today who scout out and prepare a venue in advance of an arrival. Like the farmers of yesterday, today, and tomorrow, you are expected to prepare and tend to the fields in expectation of a coming harvest.

Advance Men: As such, we are tasked to go out and survey the area to see if all that is required for the advent is available in that area. These advance men should make note of the facilities that are available and the tasks that need to be done, preparing the area so that all will go smoothly at the time of arrival. They are also supposed to line up those who can help prepare the appropriate venue and set the atmosphere for the coming event.

Heralds: As heralds we are tasked with alerting and preparing the populace with correct information about the impending arrival of the coming King. We are to tell the story of the expected personage and should be prepared to answer questions about the arrival and the event. We are expected to understand and be thoroughly familiar with what is written in the Bible so that we won't give false understandings of the expected one and His message. All the while, we should be checking to see that the advance men have performed adequately and have set in motion all the work that needs to be done so that when the day arrives, all will go smoothly.

Farmers: Then while the advance men and heralds are doing this, we are to be getting the fields ready to accept and nurture the seed. Then planting the seed. We are expected to water, cultivate and tend the fields to bring our crops to maturity. Then in expectation of the coming harvest, we are to get ready by ensuring that there enough workers for the arrival of the harvest.

All these things are simple to do and yet they are needed. We are tasked with going out, surveying the fields, and working to prepare the way for the coming of our Lord. We are to be seeing to the announcement of His coming and informing the populace of His glory.

> "Listen! It's the voice of someone shouting, "Clear the way through the wilderness for the LORD! Make a straight highway through the wasteland for our God!"
> ~ Isaiah 40:3

We have our instructions, our hopes and our expectations. What we cannot do is ignore them, nor can we just sit by and wait. We need to choose which of these functions we are called to fulfill; better yet we are called to perform all, to varying levels.

Like Elijah and John the Baptist, we are tasked with declaring His coming, His expectations, and all the while calling people to Him.

> "I'm thunder in the desert: 'Make the road straight for God!' I'm doing what the prophet Isaiah preached."
> ~ John 1:23

Are we thundering? Thunder need not be deafening it can be the low rumbling warning of a coming storm. Are we clearing and smoothing the road ahead for Him? Are we getting ourselves and others ready for all to welcome Him?

Essay: Transformation

When we say the word *transformation*, very often we imagine something spectacular and instantaneous with inescapable very visible changes. Is it that really what transformation is? Or is it actually, more of a turning away from the old ways that grows from within, a turning away from that which previously had entertained our thoughts and time? Could it actually be a slow, growing change in our attitudes and perspectives? We, especially today, look for instantaneous changes. The problem there is that an instantaneous change is rarely a permanent one and often requires outside coercion or force which many times engenders resentment and rebellion. This reluctant transformation is only surface change not a lasting heart habit or character growth. To become a heart habit in the Biblical sense it must involve not only the feeling of sensing the rightness, but it should engage the mind in understanding the rightness, the body in performing and speaking the right, and finally the will in continuing in the right. When the change is not done from the "heart" the overt evil has merely been plastered over with a pretty facade, but it still simmers below the surface. Any true transformation is a slow process of choices, conviction, and growth.

Are we in need of transformation? Most definitely! Can we force transformation on one another? Most definitely **not**! To be transformed each must be convinced of the need and willing to do the hard work to make the changes on their own. Yes, we can force others to conform to our way of doing things but have we transformed them? No, not so much. We do not transform anyone in this manner, they are just following along the path of least resistance. They have not understood or owned for themselves the need for a life change. In a word there has been no change of heart nor a turning toward God with its turning away from the ways of the world.

In the Bible it is recorded the circumstances of just how much in need of transformation Israel was approximately six hundred years before the Messiah's coming. Below, you will find a listing of the conditions that God said were in need of transformation. Amazingly, these same conditions could have been torn from today's news headlines: oppression, rebellion, disgraceful acts, and thoughts, degraded morals, abusive actions, distrustful, rejection, arrogance, deceit, pride, being unprincipled, treachery, disrespecting just law, profane words and actions, and violence in words and deeds. Ouch, we haven't transformed much after all these years have we! God had his prophet Zephaniah declare this indictment of His people, included in it was a warning that contained reminders about the past consequences He had meted out as well as the promises He, God, had given to the Israelites. The indictment concludes with His promise of restoration when they would choose to honoring God's ways. The entire accounting, reminders and promise can be found in the third chapter of the book Zephaniah.

> "Woe to the city of oppressors, rebellious and defiled! She obeys no one, she accepts no correction. She does not trust in the LORD, she does not draw near to her God. Her officials within her are roaring lions; her rulers are evening wolves, who leave nothing for the morning. Her prophets are unprincipled; they are treacherous people. Her priests profane the sanctuary and do violence to the law. The LORD within her is righteous; he does no wrong. Morning by morning he dispenses his justice, and every new day he does not fail, yet the unrighteous know no shame."
> ~ Zephaniah 3: 1-5

Again, it is eerie just how contemporary these accusations are! Today our unrighteous blatantly display their contempt for proper behavior demanding acceptance for their actions. Did God forcefully impose the corrections on the people? No, He pointed out the problems, issued a reminder of what He had done in the past, and stated a warning about what consequences were impending should they choose not to change. As His word is just and true, He would then follow through and allow the consequences to play out should the people choose not to heed the warning.

> "I have destroyed nations; their strongholds are demolished. I have left their streets deserted, with no one passing through. Their cities are laid waste; they are deserted and empty."
> ~ Zephaniah 3: 6

Let us not be like the Israel of old, of whom God said, "I thought you would listen to instruction and correction. I thought you would repent of your ways and return to me!" Let us look to ourselves, then seek His instruction and make every attempt to transform our ways. His word still stands and the justice He delivers is unchanging. We are not going to be held responsible for the heart changes of those around us just our own heart changes and a willingness to provide others with the information and opportunity to choose the same for themselves.

> "Of Jerusalem I thought, 'Surely you will fear me and accept correction!' Then her place of refuge would not be destroyed, nor all my punishments come upon her. But they were still eager to act corruptly in all they did. Therefore, wait for me," declares the LORD, "for the day I will stand up to testify." I have decided to assemble the nations, to gather the kingdoms and to pour out my wrath on them all my fierce anger. The whole world will be consumed by the fire of my jealous anger."
> ~ Zephaniah 3: 7, 8

Although God says "I will", this purification happens only through the free will choice made by the remnant people to accept, follow, and adhere to the principles and precepts. While we, being the impatient creatures that we are, want it instantaneously, it is only over a period of time that the transformation occurs. It is in the turning from that which is evil in God's eye and accepting the gift that He has proffered that we are transformed. For nothing we could do of our own accord could make sufficient restitution for the mistakes we have made. He offers a clean slate on which to write, he offers forgiveness when our shortcomings prevail. We have been given innumerable second chances to do better. Sadly, until we can emulate Christ to perfection, I doubt we will ever get it (righteousness) exactly as it is required.

"Then I will purify the lips of the peoples, That all of them may call on the name of the LORD And serve him shoulder to shoulder. From beyond the rivers of Cush my worshipers, My scattered people, will bring me offerings. On that day you, Jerusalem, will not be put to shame For all the wrongs you have done to me, Because I will remove from you your arrogant boasters. Never again will you be haughty on my holy hill. But I will leave within you the meek and humble. The remnant of Israel will trust in the name of the LORD. They will do no wrong; They will tell no lies. A deceitful tongue will not be found in their mouths. They will eat and lie down and no one will make them afraid." "Sing, Daughter Zion; shout aloud, Israel! Be glad and rejoice with all your heart, Daughter Jerusalem! The LORD has taken away your punishment, He has turned back your enemy. The LORD, the King of Israel, is with you; Never again will you fear any harm. On that day they will say to Jerusalem, "Do not fear, Zion; Do not let your hands hang limp. The LORD your God is with you, The Mighty Warrior who saves. He will take great delight in you; In his love he will no longer rebuke you, But will rejoice over you with singing. I will remove from you all who mourn Over the loss of your appointed festivals, Which is a burden and reproach for you. At that time I will deal with all who oppressed you. I will rescue the lame; I will gather the exiles. I will give them praise and honor in every

> land Where they have suffered shame.
> At that time I will gather you; At that time
> I will bring you home. I will give you
> honor and praise Among all the peoples of
> the earth When I restore your fortunes
> before your very eyes," Says the LORD."
> ~ Zephaniah 3: 9-20

The above accounting, warning, and promise was written some six hundred years before the Advent of Christ. Again, it seems that man would, again, merit the same indictment. Mankind is, certainly, in as much need of the very same warning today as the charges against him would almost be precisely the same as more than two thousand six hundred years ago. Perhaps we should learn from Israel's history; for the consequences are still as dire, yet the prospect of God's promise remains.

> "Create me a clean heart, O God;
> And renew a steadfast spirit within me."
> - Psalms 51:12

This transformation starts with our willingness to accept that we are not the sole controlling force in our lives. Then concede, that as totally undeserving as we are; we are the recipients of a cleansing from all of our stains and that all of our debts have been cleared. It is just our pride and independent spirit that stand in our way towards making this transformation.

A Season of Gladness

We have been given tidings of exceedingly great gladness! We have the honor and joy of accepting and sharing these tidings, which should fill us with a great sense of delight. The light that has come shines with a brightness that illuminates the world with His loving gift. The great weight of our inability to achieve perfection has been removed relieving the anxiety and fear that we might not succeed in what we try. This should fill us with a wondrous sense lightness.

"You, Lord, are my lamp; The Lord turns
my darkness into light."
~ 2 Samuel 22: 29

With Advent, we will extol this enlightening that came for all the world with great celebrations, appreciation, and jubilation, for with the birth of Jesus the whole of creation was made glad. The task given to us, we (who have seen the light and are willing to accept what it offers); then to invite all to join us in the gladness that this gift brings. Doing this with expressions of great joy!

"For all the gods of the nations are idols,
But the Lord made the heavens. Splendor
and majesty are before him; Strength and
joy are in his dwelling place. Ascribe to
the Lord, all you families of nations,
Ascribe to the Lord Glory and strength."
~ 1 Chronicles 16: 26-28

Essay: Illumination

"You, Lord, keep my lamp burning;
my God turns my darkness into light."
~ Psalm 18:28

What a shining happiness has come into the world! Yet when the light first dawns within our hearts and minds though, initially, it is very disconcerting. Since many, if not all, of us are somewhat self-absorbed, our first look would be at ourselves. If we look in honesty, making a comparison between what we have become and the standard that God has given us for what we should be; we experience a revulsion. Our first reaction would be to hide away in darkness ashamed of what we see in ourselves. This would be wrong, for to be in total darkness is unnerving, disorienting, and it obscures what we need to see. Instead, we should turn to the light and look at the gift of God for the forgiveness of our debts and the cleansing from all of our failings. This gift that we have done nothing to earn but has been offered to us out of a great Love. Then, if we are honest, we acknowledge there is nothing we are capable of doing that would even come close to the value of what has been freely given. When we then take the leap of faith and accept this gift that is being offered, we experience a lifting of our spirits and soul that shines with an almost blinding light. This lighting comes not only with a new found clarity of vision and understanding, but also, an incredible lifting of the weight from our soul's being brought about by the incredible mercy and grace that has come to us. For all too long, we have depended on our own or the devices of others to lift us. Time and again have been let down or disappointed. All too often, we have found ourselves in the places we were warned about, stumbling around and searching for ways out of messes of our own, or others', making.

> "At midday you will grope about like a blind man in the dark. You will be unsuccessful in everything you do; day after day you will be oppressed and robbed, with no one to rescue you."
> ~ Deuteronomy 28:29

We now realize that have been given proof that God has been watching over us and loving us, all of the time. That His yearnings for his stubborn and stumbling children would find expression in such a wondrous way is awe inspiring and humbling. When the time was right, He promised that He would place before us the opportunity for returning and forgiveness, and He has. This realization lifts a great darkness from our hearts! He has told us countless times that at the right time, He would search us out, rescue us from the predicaments we had gotten ourselves into, strengthen us, heal us and return us to His companionship.

Here is one of the many lists of what God has promised His children. It is a listing of how He wishes to care for His people written down for us to hold on to and ponder. This listing provides us a reassurance as we strive to emulate the one who has loved us so thoroughly that He does not expect perfection immediately. I have underlined those promises which I consider as good cause for our sense of confidence and happiness.

> "As a shepherd looks after his scattered flock when he is with them, so will I look after my sheep. I will rescue them from all the places where they were scattered on a day of clouds and darkness. I will bring them out from the nations and gather them from the countries, and I will bring them into their own land. I will pasture them on the mountains of Israel, in the ravines and in all the settlements in the land. I will tend them in a good pasture, and the mountain heights of Israel will be their grazing land. There they will lie down in good grazing land, and there they will feed

> in a rich pasture on the mountains of Israel. I myself will tend my sheep and have them lie down, declares the Sovereign Lord. I will search for the lost and bring back the strays. I will bind up the injured and strengthen the weak, but the sleek and the strong I will destroy. I will shepherd the flock with justice."
> ~ Ezekiel 34: 12-16

Oh let us commemorate this dawning Advent light, with rejoicing in the love that made it possible! Let the light that has come to the World enter in, cleanse the windows of our souls, and provide illumination to each of us so that we may become what each was made to be. Let us celebrate and share this light that shines within us with the world.

Essay: Celebration

> "The people who walk in darkness will see
> a great light. For those who live in a land
> of deep darkness, a light will shine."
> ~ Isaiah 9:2

We have been given this great light. It still shines out to the world and is still beckoning to everyone. Is that not enough of a reason to celebrate? This light communicates to us that the sought after relief from all that which weighs us down and holds us prisoner is at hand. It, also, is the happy response welling up from within caused by the offer of freedom from our sense of guilt and shame that keeps us from approaching God gladly. Before this gift, it was imperative to perform a yearly ritual of repentance. This yearly ritual repentance had to precisely follow the steps ordained. This was not a once and done ritual but had to be performed three times [once for the high priest, once for the priesthood and leadership, and once again for the people] each year, to obtain this grace from our errors. Then this ritual would only cover us for the errors and sins committed in the preceding year to be repeated again the next year. Under this old system we had to plead for this mercy. Now it is available to all as a gift, free for the asking. Now we no longer need make supplication via an intermediary, we can approach Him directly in confidence that we will be heard and that what is best for us shall be provided. Should we not dance, sing, and hug those around us in a celebration of great gladness?

> "Bring my soul out of prison, that I may
> celebrate your name. The righteous shall
> surround me, because you deal bountifully
> with me."
> ~ Psalm 142:7

It was so, promised, and it was so, delivered! Is this not another wonderful cause for a great celebration in recognition of the honor, the faithfulness, and the truthfulness of God? Even though we have failed to live up to our side of the covenants with God, we have proof that He still abides in His word. He has made the way to bring our souls out of the prisons we have found ourselves in. This is a great relief to all, and lifts the great burden from our shoulders. Here is another reason for a great celebration!

> "Jehovah, thou art my God: I will exalt
> thee; I will celebrate thy name, for thou
> hast done wonderful things; counsels of
> old which are faithfulness and truth."
> - Isaiah 25:1 (ASV)

So, in this season of celebration and all subsequent days, have we not an immense cause to rejoice? Our debts and errors have been paid for. Should we not acknowledge this love and accept the gift that has been offered with great celebrations. Yes, and with Advent we gratefully acknowledge and celebrate this gift.

> "You will have a song, as in the night
> when a holy feast is kept; and you will be
> glad in heart, as when they go with music
> of the pipe to the mountain of the Lord, the
> Rock of Israel."
> - Isaiah 30:29

The Seasons of Advent

Essay: Appreciation

Appreciation, a sentiment that, we humans seem to be rather poor at expressing in any lasting and genuine manner. We tend more often to fixate on the confusions, hurts, and grievances in our lives rather than on the considerations, kindnesses, blessings, and gifts that have been given to us. It is ironic then, that one of the biggest wounds we complain about, is the lack of appreciation given to us by others for our own small efforts when we ourselves take for granted the greatest gift that has ever been given to us!

We think that we want to be the center of our own universes. Consider, is that truly where we want to be? Do we ever stop to think of all it means to be in that position? If we did, it would most likely be decided we would not really want to be there? The centers of the universes, galaxies, and even planets are the places where the greatest concentrations of heat, pressure, and stress are found. Is this really where we want to be? In the grand scheme of things we were not placed in the center but at just the right distance out, where there is a balance suitable to sustaining life. Because of the vastness of the universe, we posit that we are not in the sole location where life could found. But for all our searching, we've yet to positively identify another location. We were, also, not made to be the center of control, assuming the responsibility for the entirety of creation. We were given the stewardship position, responsible to the Creator for that portion which He has given to us as our responsibility. It is not our responsibility to create the plan and insure its implementation. The order that is evident throughout points to the thoughtful consideration, planning, and design God gave to His creation. We should hold this as a blessing to be thankful for as it would be overwhelming to be held accountable for proper function of the entire Creation.

The psalmist wrote of this wonder and awe in Psalm 8.

> "O LORD, our Lord, How majestic is
> Your name in all the earth, Who have
> displayed Your splendor above the

> heavens! From the mouth of infants and nursing babes You have established strength Because of Your adversaries, To make the enemy and the revengeful cease. When I consider Your heavens, the work of Your fingers, The moon and the stars, which You have ordained; What is man that You take thought of him, And the son of man that You care for him?"

What is appreciation? First, it is a recognition. Secondly it is a favorable evaluation. Lastly (and most importantly), it is an expression of gratitude for the consideration, kindness, gift, or grace that has been made available for everyone. For all that our Holy God and Creator has done, even when we've gone our own ways out of curiosity, stubbornness, and pride, do we show appreciation His forbearance and love? He has warned, chastised, instructed, and made a path for our return when we have wandered. Are we thankful? He has even promised to welcome us back no matter how vile we've been. For this alone we should be grateful! Appreciation! It is the very least we should give!

The Seasons of Advent

Essay: Jubilation

"In the seventh month,
on the first day of the month,
you shall observe
a day of solemn rest,
a memorial proclamation
with a blast of trumpets,
a holy convocation."
~ Leviticus 23: 24

From the beginning the number seven has had a significance and meaning that contains blessing to all of God's creation. The number carries a sense of completeness, significance, and blessing in it and its multiples that are beyond my comprehension. Starting from God's declaration on the seventh day that no further work need be done for creation as it was now complete. The Hebrew word translated as rest has the connotation of satisfaction in a work well and truly complete. Then the seventh day was given to His creation as a day of rest and physical restoration. Later, the seventh month was given to us as a month of remembrance and spiritual restoration for us to make atonement. The seventh (sabbatical) year was instituted by God as a year of rest and restoration for all the land. Finally, after the seventh sabbatical year an entire year was set aside and designated as the year of Jubilee!

We get our word *jubilation* from the Latin word meaning to shout with great joy. The word *jubilee*, also, is a transliteration of the Hebrew name of the horn (Yobhel) used to announce the beginning of a year given to forgiveness and restoration. This year, God prescribed for granting of forgiveness comes every fiftieth year. The Yobhel is to be sounded throughout the land at the commencement of the year on the Day of Atonement. What was to happen during the year of Jubilee? There was to be a return to one's original standing within the community, forgiveness of debts and freedom from slavery. During that time God assured Israel that He would provide sufficiency for all be available directly from the bounty of the fields by God's provision.

All this seems to be pointing to a later restoration of greater significance, a restoration to a right standing with God, by a sufficient provision from the Lord. Its proscribed order is significant to me as well. The order is as follows:

- hearing the announcement of the coming,
- the preparations of cleansing,
- the receiving of a covering of atonement,
- the receiving of forgiveness for all debts and freedom from slavery, and
- entering into a return to a right standing before God. Is this not the process that still exists for each of us as we enter into a relationship with Christ? First we hear of Him, then we prepare to accept Him, and we, then, receive His grace and His mercy. Most of us have accepted the gift, we are now working at cleaning our hearts as we prepare for His return for His bride. We have been made free and await the complete return to our standing with God. Can you think of any greater reason for shouts of great joy than this?

The following psalm is what the psalmist wrote of celebrating the year of Great Jubilee. He wrote:

> "O sing to the LORD a new song, For He has done wonderful things, His right hand and His holy arm have gained the victory for Him. The LORD has made known His salvation; He has revealed His righteousness in the sight of the nations. He has remembered His loving-kindness and His faithfulness to the house of Israel; All the ends of the earth have seen the salvation of our God. Shout joyfully to the LORD, all the earth; Break forth and sing

The Seasons of Advent

for joy and sing praises. Sing praises to the LORD with the lyre, With the lyre and the sound of melody, with trumpets and the sound of the horn, shout joyfully before the King, the LORD. Let the sea roar and all it contains, The world and those who dwell in it. Let the rivers clap their hands, Let the mountains sing together for joy. Before the LORD, for He is coming to judge the earth; He will judge the world with righteousness And the peoples with equity."
~ Psalm 98

The ram's horn, shofar, reminds us of the substitutionary sacrifice provided by God in Genesis of the ram for Abraham son. This event prefigures the substitutionary sacrifice that would be made for all mankind. This horn is first referenced in the giving of the Law on Mount Sinai (the first Shofar blast) as a call to return to righteousness, and it is thought to be what Jesus will sound at the "Last Trumpet" calling his children home. With the sounding of the trumpet (shofar) at the beginning of worship, we are reminded of several things that God has promised to His people as well as of what is expected of us. Among these are a call to repentance, coming of God's judgments, God's enthronement, and divine mercy, and remembrance; lastly it reminds us that he will be calling us home. With these promises in mind, great will be our jubilation at the sound of God's trumpet calling us to his freedom and love.

A Season of Promise

> "He remembers his covenant forever,
> the promise he made, for a thousand
> generations,"
> ~ 1 Chronicles 16: 15

Advent is, most of all, a season in which we honor and celebrate the fulfillment of God's greatest promise to the world. Since the beginning he declared to mankind that he would expect certain things, perform certain things, and provide certain things. Through the ages he has proven these declarations over and over. If we know what he has said we can live in the confidence of his promises because he has proven himself over and over and over again.

Because He is who He is, we, through His greatest act of love, have been given the opportunity to accept the forbearance, leadings, and grace He promised to humanity so long ago. It, also, gives us a confident sense of assurance in the successful outcome of all His pronouncements. It includes the knowledge that though we may not see the conclusion or understand the way they will come into being; we can have the confidence that the end will be perfect and excellent.

> "How I long for your precepts! In your
> righteousness preserve my life. May your
> unfailing love come to me, Lord, your
> salvation, according to your promise; then
> I can answer anyone who taunts me, for I
> trust in your word."
> ~ Psalm 119: 40-42

Essay: <u>**Constant**</u>

> As He has done in the past; we can have the complete confidence He will continue to do now and forever! "God is not a man, that he should lie; neither the son of man, that he should repent: hath he said, and shall he not do it? or hath he spoken, and shall he not make it good?"
> ~ Numbers 23:19 (KJV)

In this season we can embrace this promise God made, that He is ever constant and true to His word. Since the first stumbling of man, God has been constant to His given word. This includes not only His words which were given in His covenants with mankind to provide for a restoration for those who have stumbled, He, also, considers binding all of his promises and pronouncements. Yes, there were periods when man was left to suffer the consequences of our actions and choices that broke our portion of the covenants. Yet through it all God has remained constant and has graciously restored those who returned to Him through repentance. This gives all who look to God, something very solid and stable to build our lives around and a sturdy base from which we can reach outward to others. This promise gives His people a calm surety that is the marvel of those around them as the storms of life rage.

For He has declared solemnly to us that:

> "I will not violate my covenant
> or alter what my lips have uttered."
> ~ Psalm 89:34

One of His main promises is that He would provide a way for our reconciliation and restoration. All His plans and actions toward fulfilling this promise give evidence of his love for mankind. This, constancy, is an indication just how much God regards the companionship of the only portion of creation for which He has said:

> "So God created mankind in his own
> image, in the image of God he created
> them; male and female he created them."
> ~ Genesis 1:27

The first step toward this reconciliation and restoration was through the giving of the Law so that we would be made fully aware of the requirements for entering into his presence. While man has made many attempts on his own, he has fallen woefully short of the perfection required to enter into God's presence and has suffered many occasions of estrangement and exile. Each time God has restored them upon evidence of repentance.

During one such restoration, as recorded in the Bible, even the names of those involved point to the promise of continued offers of reconciliation. In the past people were given names that expressed a belief, a hope, an ideal desired, or a commemoration of an event. Thus, they had meaning beyond just a given label of a given person. An example of this is can be found within this verse from the book of Ezra from the time of the restoration of Israel to Jerusalem from its long exile in Babylon.

Ezra 10:2:

> Then Shekaniah son of Jehiel, one of the descendants of Elam, said to Ezra, "We have been unfaithful to our God by marrying foreign women from the peoples around us. But in spite of this, there is still hope for Israel.

If one expands out the meanings of the given names and one term within the verse, it reads as a promise of future help and hope. So it might read thusly:

> Then he who God has taken His abode with the son of him, who was carried away by Him, descended out of the hidden time and sent a strong vision of help said. "We have been unfaithful to our LORD and have taken to ignorant things from the people around us, yet now there is hope for God strives concerning these things. [1].

This demonstrates that in God's economy even the given names of His chosen participants can carry His message to mankind.

Essay: Guidance

> "In your unfailing love you will lead the
> people you have redeemed. In your
> strength you will guide them to your holy
> dwelling."
> ~ Exodus 15:13

God is our guide, not a drover. A guide is one who leads, instructs, and encourages his charges towards a destination. While a drover is one who drives his charges along by force or coercion to get them where he desire by the strength of his will. With God, He desires that we are allowed to choose to follow or not to follow.

I'm reminded of a story about a farmer who had several cows that he wished to move from one field to another. His friends offered to help him drive the cattle where he wanted but he declined remarking that this would only agitate the cows. Instead, he got his feed pail and rattled it as he led the way from one field to another. Most of the herd followed along at the time and went smoothly from the old field into the new one. One cow, however, did not. The farmer calmly closed the gate and waited awhile. Sure enough the "rebel" without being forced soon presented herself at the gate.

God, much like the farmer of the story, shows us the way, while presenting us with the needed information and allowing us to make the choice. He gives us His guidance and encouragement all along our journey with Him. The choice offered; is to come along with Him or to go our own way. Yet God also provides the option for those who stray to repent and follow along later.

> "By day the Lord went ahead of them in a
> pillar of cloud to guide them on their way"
> ~ Exodus 13:21

This instance of God's guidance has been recorded for us as an instructional reminder and an example of how God will show us the way. At this time God wanted to bring his chosen people (and those who chose Him) to their promised home. When the offer was made, most, but not all, chose to follow. Some of those remaining behind chose later to follow. While there were some, after starting out on the journey had second thoughts about the difficulties of their choice and at several points in the journey, some of these even turned back and returned to Egypt.

At other times, God has given us signs and events to watch for along our way. These were to let us be aware that God was about to move in our lives and fulfill a promise that had been given. One such time that Israel was given a guide post to watch for is found in the book of Numbers chapter 22. It was delivered by the prophet Balaam. After several failed attempts to curse Israel at the behest of their enemy King Balaak of Moab, he submitted to God's will and prophesied about Israel's coming Messiah, saying.

> "I see him, but not now; I behold him, but not near. A star will come out of Jacob; a scepter will rise out of Israel."
> ~ Numbers 24:17

Israel was given this guide post to watch for along their journey through time. This guide post was recorded well before Israel went into exile into Babylon the first time. It is odd, though when the time came, that the only ones diligently watching for this sign were not the Israelites but the gentile Magi. Later, this prophecy was elaborated upon and refined in texts that narrowed down the places we were to be watching.

In one passage, man through Israel, was told where the Messiah would appear yet when asked by the gentiles about His announced arrival the reference was not readily called to mind and had to be searched out. This is strange because at the time the Magi were asking for further information was, also, a time when many in Israel were at least talking about their desire for the promised Messiah.

> "But you, Bethlehem Ephrathah, though
> you are small among the clans of Judah,
> out of you will come for me one who will
> be ruler over Israel, whose origins are from

of old, from ancient times."
~ Micah 5:2

In another verse, what the coming Messiah would be like was foretold, yet still the Israelites looked for, and some feared a political and military leader, not one who would refresh and reawaken the Spirit within us. This Messiah, Jesus, made the leadership of Israel (the priests, scribes and nobility) very uncomfortable with his teachings for He drew the common man into a personal relationship with God reducing their power and influence.

"And afterward, I will pour out my Spirit
on all people. Your sons and daughters will
prophesy, your old men will dream
dreams, your young men will see visions."
~ Joel 2:28

We should echo King David, with great confidence and assurance, and announce the great news that the Lord is our Shepherd. That means, for us, that God has control, gives guidance, love, provision, encouragement and dispenses justice in our lives!

"The Lord is my shepherd, I lack nothing.
He makes me lie down in green pastures,
He leads me beside quiet waters, He
refreshes my soul. He guides me along the
right paths for His name's sake. Even
though I walk through the darkest valley, I
will fear no evil, for you are with me; your
rod and your staff, they comfort me. You
prepare a table before me in the presence
of my enemies. You anoint my head with
oil; my cup overflows. Surely your
goodness and love will follow me all the
days of my life, and I will dwell in the
house of the Lord forever."
~ Psalm 23

Is it not wonderful that our God will still guide us with such gentleness and firmness? This is something that we can hold onto; that even when we stray, He will seek us out and point us again to paths of righteousness.

Essay: Providence

Providence: The quality or state of being careful about planning for the future. When used as Divine Providence, it has the connotation of the careful provision which God deems necessary to sustain and guide our paths should we just heed and choose. [(2)]

We should be able, if we look honestly, to answer that we truly have had what we have needed for that time provided for us. Granted, sometimes it might not have been all that we thought we desired or wanted. In fact He has always given what was sufficient for our needs. Because of who He is, who He has been and who He will always be we should be able to live confidently that He will provide precisely the right things in the right amount and in the right time!

> "You protect me with your saving shield
> [have given me the shield of your
> salvation/victory]. You support me with
> your right hand. You have stooped to make
> [Your help makes] me great."
> ~ Psalms 18: 35 (EXB)

Since the beginning He has been providing the requirements of all of His creatures, so much so, that it is one of His names; Jehovah jireh means the Lord provides. This does not imply that He will give them all of their wants or desires; but that He does give, with abundance, what is best for them. At the time of creation, for instance, man wasn't introduced until He had completed and had provisioned the perfect environment for his penultimate creation. Only then was man, the creation destined to be like unto Him and intended for companionship and union with Him, introduced.

- *The providence:* "Then God said, "I give you every seed-bearing plant on the face of the whole earth and every tree that has fruit with seed in it. They will be yours for food. And to all the beasts of the earth and all the birds in the sky and all the creatures that move along the ground -

everything that has the breath of life in it - I give every green plant for food." And it was so. God saw all that he had made, and it was very good. And there was evening, and there was morning - the sixth day." ~ Genesis 1:29-31

He, having given man free will, even made provisions from the beginning to correct the messes of his wayward creatures could and would create. He set out only one rule that was to be observed for man to remain in companionship with Him. However, all the while, knowing that as with any growing child, the boundary would be tested or broken and consequences would need to be meted out. Even in the pronouncement of that punishment He provided for the needs of man. At the same time, He hinted at the provision that would be made available in the future to us, even as he was pronouncing judgment.

> The providence: "The Lord God made garments of skin for Adam and his wife and clothed them." ~ Genesis 3:21

He could have left them with the coverings of their own devising; the fig leaves. Yet in His wisdom He provided a more thorough and lasting covering that was obtained by the blood sacrifice of one of His creations (an animal) to protect and cover the person of His creation that was made in His likeness. This hints at the cost that would come with the later provision of a complete covering of the shame that inhibits our approaching God in confidence and joy.

- The providence to come: "And I will put enmity between you and the woman, and between your offspring and hers; he will crush your head, and you will strike his heel." ~ Genesis 3:15

In this passage, from Biblical history, we are given a picture of the providence of God. First all that was needed was created before man was brought into being. In order to maintain this perfection only one rule given. God knew that in creating humans in His image, it meant, that they would not always exercise their curiosity and free-will properly. Like children the world over, they would test this one-rule limit. Knowing this, He already, had a course of action set in motion to facilitate an end to the impending estrangement. God knew that the shame that came from violating His rule would require a covering that could only be provided by Him. Finally, the hoped for reconciliation would come in the future.

Through the ages it has been seen that those who sought after God's will in most part prospered and were given guidance on how to go forward (Genesis 6-9). God has given us several pictures of what the cost to Him would be to provide the means for the universal covering that would permit the reconciliation. One such picture is presented at the inception of Israel (Genesis 22: 6-8). Later we were given the requirements that are essential in order for a person to gain access to His companionship (Exodus 20). This Law needed to be followed perfectly if we hoped achieve restoration by our own efforts. He knew all along, that above and beyond the Law, the provision for His planned gift of the covering; could only come when man had had ample evidence that they needed this gift. It would only come when we were ready to accept the grace offered in order to return to the companionship we had lost through willfulness.

> "But when the set time had fully come, God sent his Son, born of a woman, born under the law, to redeem those under the law, that we might receive adoption to sonship."
> Galatians 4:4, 5

Essay: Comfort

Oh the warm comfort, strength, and confidence that comes from knowing our Father holds us firmly by the hand as we walk through life.

> "Yet I am always with you; you hold me
> by my right hand."
> ~ Psalm 73:23

God has promised to be with those who look to Him always and to guide (teach) them throughout all their days. While at times, we would prefer that another would be assigned to do the "hard stuff" for us that is not the way of our Father. He knows what each of us needs over and above what we think we want. Yet, we should live confidently in the knowledge that He wants what is best not just what is merely good for all of His creation. We can stand in faith, knowing that His provision will be sufficient. Ultimately, it is comforting to know that while we must do the "hard things" for ourselves and while we are in the middle of the trials we may not understand where they are leading, these things will be within our strength to endure and overcome. He has, in addition, promised to walk with us through the process. The Father knows our strengths and our weaknesses above and beyond our own comprehension. It is a great comfort to know that we are part of a perfect plan, even when we cannot see the entire picture or map.

> "Think how you have instructed many,
> how you have strengthened feeble hands.
> Your words have supported those who
> stumbled; you have strengthened faltering
> knees."
> ~ Job 4: 3, 4

While enduring trials, as much as we would wish circumstances were otherwise, we find that, more often than not, when we heed His instructions, the problems before us become more manageable and we find that we can do this, in the end, we also gain the ability to reach out to others struggling with the same or similar situations. In this many of us find a value to the trials we have dealt with.

Even when we fall short and are troubled by the expected consequences, we are still promised the comfort of God's consolation and loving care. This should allow us to get up and try again that task which was asked of us, for no matter how far short we fall nor how many times we miss the mark we have been assured,

> "I will heal their waywardness and love
> them freely, for my anger has turned away
> from them."
> ~ Hosea 14:4

He has demonstrated many times that if we would just look outside of our immediate circumstances and seek Him that we find He has been with us all the time. The Bible, again, gives us this reassurance:

> "The Lord your God is with you. He is
> mighty enough to save you. He will take
> great delight in you. The quietness of his
> love will calm you down. He will sing with
> joy because of you."
> ~ Zephaniah 3:17

There is great comfort in knowing that we are loved no matter what has gone on before in our lives and a healing calm will be ours when we realize that ways of our own devising are not what is the best for us and those around us. There is a great amount of comfort, when we realize that not only have we been given the instruction we need, but also one we can run to who will know and understand us inside and out. Lastly, it is comforting to understand that in no way will our failures cut us off from the love of our Creator.

The greatest comfort of all is having our God be one who is approachable, knowable, and one who is able to understand and sympathize with our frailties. It is in this season that we celebrate this greatest of reassurances. Consider the titles bestowed on the child that has come to be our shepherd, guide and comfort:

The Seasons of Advent

> "For to us a child is born, to us a son is given, and the government will be on his shoulders. And he will be called Wonderful Counselor, Mighty God, Everlasting Father, Prince of Peace."
> ~ Isaiah 9:6

As He also reassured us, by saying,

> "Come to me, all you who are weary and burdened, and I will give you rest."
> ~ Matthew 11:28

A Season of Love:

We have said that God is love, but do we truly comprehend all that love is? A love, that is strong, that is patient, long suffering, understanding, and true, yet it also has discipline, disciplines, and is capable of wrath when this love is violated. A love that is total is one that rejoices in the growth and benefit of the beloved. A complete love also studies in order to know the innermost desires of its partner. This love is so thorough that the union appears to move as one. This is something that we all seek and desire throughout our lives. We, also, desire a love that perseveres but does not compel by force, one that is willing to let us go albeit with great sorrow.

Advent is the celebration of the fact that God has loved us in this manner, and he has continually modeled it. He has modeled this love so thoroughly in that He left behind His home and went to the far place where we had wandered. He, then offered himself as the total payment for every single one of our debts, omissions and crimes. When this was accomplished, He then said to us, "Come home" but He does not force us to go.

Then as if His example were not enough, God also gave us a perfect description of this love. It can be found in 1 Corinthians, so it is available to refresh our memory any time we need reminder.

> "Love is patient, love is kind. It does not
> envy, it does not boast, it is not proud. It
> does not dishonor others, it is not self-
> seeking, it is not easily angered, it keeps no

> record of wrongs. Love does not delight in
> evil but rejoices with the truth. It always
> protects, always trusts, always hopes,
> always perseveres. Love never fails."
> ~ 1 Corinthians 13: 4-8

Also, this love does not accept counterfeit return nor does it give whatever the loved one desires, especially if the desire is detrimental to the well-being of the loved one. Much to our dismay, at times, discipline or lessons need to be applied and learned. We can be confident that until the lesson we need to learn for our growth is well and truly incorporated, God in His love will place the lesson before us again.

Essay: Persevering

The true meaning of *perseverance* is to continue despite difficulties and opposition. God has had to deal with his creation's blunderings and willful stubborn disobedience in its handling of his most wonderful and singular gift; the gift of a free will. From the beginning, man has struggled to appropriately handle this gift and to deal with the consequences of when his decisions do not come up to the perfection required. Yet through it all God has persevered in loving kindness to bring us back into the fellowship that was enjoyed at the time of creation. He has shown us time and again the most excellent ways. Yet he does not force any one person to select these paths. Rather, throughout all of time God has come seeking after his straying fold to guide them back to the right path.

Even after the disastrous consequences of the fall in the Garden of Eden, did God cut off all contact with people? No, he continued to walk and talk with them [3]; even the ones who had violated [4] His instructions. God does not want any of His creations to be eternally lost. Even when we hesitate, He reaches out to us [5] to take our hand and help us to safety.

Even when man's rebelliousness had so soiled God's creation that wiping the slate clean to begin again was an option; a single man (Noah – Genesis 6) who sought His face was enough to forestall that option. Again and again, we have received the grace to try again. Each time instructions were given to show us what was required for us to gain access to Him. Each time, like the good shepherd He has sought out the lost and seeking ones. He, then, has guided them back to the path.

During Advent, we celebrate the fact God once again deigned to walk and talk with mankind on earth for a time. We are made glad that He continues to seek and save the lost and wandering. We rejoice with great celebrations that He came to give us instruction, to guide us to repentance, once more to lead us in the paths pleasing to God, and to offer us a grace once and for all, providing an all-sufficient covering for all of our stumblings and rebellions.

The purpose that has been in place since our eviction from Eden has been told to us from the lips of the one who traveled so far to offer us the opportunity of Salvation.

> "Jesus said to him, "Today salvation has
> come to this house, because this man, too,
> is a son of Abraham. For the Son of Man
> came to seek and to save the lost."
> ~ Luke 19: 9, 10

Essay: Faithful

> "Know therefore that the Lord your God is
> God; he is the <u>faithful</u> God, <u>keeping</u> his
> covenant of love to a thousand generations
> of those who love him and keep his
> commandments."
> ~ Deuteronomy 7:9

Our God has declared himself to be a covenant keeper time and again. A covenant agreement is binding to all parties, but above that, its conditions remain binding on the remaining party even if the other party has broken their portion of the covenant. That means that even when we do not uphold our side of the covenant, God will still uphold his portion. So it is that we may depend on God faithfully upholding what He has promised to mankind within the Covenants, no matter how faithless we have been to our promises time and again.

In my understanding, there were been three covenants made between God and mankind in the Old Testament. The very first one was made with mankind, in total, and the latter two were made with Israel specifically. Each covenant contained elements that were purposed for returning mankind to fellowship with God. The fourth covenant was established in the New Testament by Jesus. This New Covenant when established, granted individual access in communion with God and is much like a betrothal promise of union. Each one of the first three was later elaborated to tell how this New Covenant was to be fulfilled. There has been the Noahic, the Abrahamic, and the Mosaic covenants, and during Advent we celebrate the inauguration of the fourth covenant. In the Noahic, we see a sheltering from the storms and a separation from the worldly things and the promise of future sheltering. The Abrahamic Covenant, shows us the selection and separation by faith that is elemental to our relationship. The Mosaic Covenant, tells of the righteousness and right dealings that are required to obtain free and complete access with God. The Mosaic Covenant is, also, the mechanism by which we come to see just how much we need the gift of grace that will be made available with the institution of the New Covenant. With the Advent of Jesus Christ comes the New Covenant which was foretold to the Prophet Jeremiah. This last Covenant signifies that in one person the first three were completed entering into a new way to relate to and with God.

With each Covenant, God gave us a sign to reassure us that His covenant remains in force and that He will continue to honor His word. The rainbow was given to us as the sign that the Noahic Covenant remains in force. Circumcision was given to Israel as a sign of separation from the standards of the world as a part of the Abrahamic Covenant. The sign that was provided to Israel for the Mosaic Covent were the ten laws that were engraved by the hand of God into stone signifying their permanence.

Some five hundred years before Christ, we were told by the prophet Jeremiah that there would come a time when God would institute a new covenant that would be unlike the previous ones.

> "The days are coming," declares the Lord, "when I will make a <u>new covenant</u> with the people of Israel and with the people of Judah. It will not be like the covenant I made with their ancestors when I took them by the hand to lead them out of Egypt, because they broke my covenant, though I was a husband to them," declares the Lord. "This is the covenant I will make with the people of Israel after that time," declares the Lord. "I will put my law in their minds and write it on their hearts. I will be their God, and they will be my people. No longer will they teach their neighbor, or say to one another, 'Know the Lord,' because they will all know me, from the least of them to the greatest," declares the Lord. "For I will forgive their wickedness and will remember their sins no more."
> ~ Jeremiah 31: 31-34

As a sign that the fourth covenant, the New Covenant, was now in force Our Lord instituted the Meal of Communion with God. This meal, symbolized by the breaking of bread and partaking of the cup commemorates all that was accomplished with Jesus' Advent and the promise of His expected return.

> "While they were eating, Jesus took bread, and when he had given thanks, he broke it and gave it to his disciples, saying, "Take and eat; this is my body." Then he took a cup, and when he had given thanks, he gave it to them, saying, "Drink from it, all of you. This is my blood of the new covenant, which is poured out for many for the forgiveness of sins."
> ~ Matthew 26: 26-28

In essence, all of these covenants are in fact part of God's singular plan of returning His creation to a personal and daily loving relationship with Him. So during Advent we celebrate the faithful fulfillment of his promises and can rest in confidence upon the knowledge of God's constancy throughout all time.

Side note: throughout the Bible there is a sense of a very stable solidity that is implied in the number four. For examples of completion: four seasons completing the cycle of a year, the fourth day of creation saw the completion of the material world. There is the solid stability symbolized in the square that continues in today's usage indicates a completeness as in four square and square meal

Essay: Forgiving

Our God is not only a God of forgiveness, but he is also one who is very eager to grant us the healing of a complete forgiveness. He has a great yearning over our stubbornness and longs for us to return to Him. One of the greatest stories that illustrates how His eagerness to forgive us is found in the parable told by Jesus of the lost sons (Luke 15: 11-32). Most of us know this as the parable of the Prodigal Son, but in this parable, God also demonstrates a prodigality of forgiveness and provision for both of his sons. First let us understand the word *prodigal*. It has two connotations that can be seen as opposites. The more commonly understood meaning is the one of seemingly wasteful extravagance which some might argue are the failings of both sons in this story. The older squanders the love and fellowship of the Father for a perceived future standing and material benefits and the younger squanders the material goods that the Father provided for immediate gratification. The other side of the word connotes providing in luxurious abundance. This abundance is evident in the lavish celebration given to celebrate the repentance and return of the younger son and the concern that drew the Father to attempt to bring the elder son into the rejoicing. Throughout the story the reader has the sense of the Father's yearning for a U-turn in thinking for both of His children. The turn is obvious for the one that had sought other things away from the Father, it is less obvious with the son who had conformed on the surface but had remained only for the material gain in the future. This yearning is so strong that the Father does not stand on his dignity, nor require proper ceremony or penance but runs to the repentant one upon the visible evidence of return.

Another example of God's eager willingness to forgive not only his chosen people who were to bear his message to the world, but is inclusive of all peoples is found in the story of Jonah. The prophet Jonah had been tasked with carrying God's warning message to repent to Nineveh. God sent him to warn them, so that they might be spared the dire consequences of their actions. The people of Nineveh were feared and hated for the brutality of their practices in that day so Jonah was very reluctant to offer them this saving opportunity. When the Ninevites took God's message to heart and repented, God relented in His intent to punish the people Nineveh. Jonah was irate, and, in today's parlance, said "That's not fair!" Jonah as recorded says to God,

> "But to Jonah this seemed very wrong, and
> he became angry. He prayed to the Lord,
> "Isn't this what I said, Lord, when I was
> still at home? That is what I tried to
> forestall by fleeing to Tarshish. I knew that
> you are a gracious and compassionate God,
> slow to anger and abounding in love, a
> God who relents from sending calamity."
> ~ Jonah 4: 1, 2

When God showers his forgiveness on the sinning, like Jonah we tend to sulk when things go other than the way we think they should. Should we not remember that our understanding and grasp of the total picture is limited? Sometimes our understanding of what is just gets mixed up with retribution, not repentance.

The Father so wants to forgive everyone that He sent His Son to clear the path, pay our debts, and remove the chains that bind us. It is in this Advent, that we find our greatest opportunity for release from the bondage of our errors. It is this Advent that expresses the depth of God's yearning to forgive his children and to accept them back into companionship and communion.

Essay: <u>**True**</u>

* Steadfast
* Honest
* Just
* Consistent

These are just a few of the words that are used to define the word *true*. They are also essential descriptions of the character of God. In fancy terms, He is omniscient, omnipresent, and omnipotent, and enduring. Omniscient assures us that nothing is out of His understanding and wisdom. Omnipresent means that nothing escapes nor can it escape His notice and awareness. Omnipotent gives us the confidence that nothing is impossible to Him. Enduring assures us that what was, is still today and will be forever. These words are ones that we can hold on to in complete confidence and security. With Christ, they became approachable and welcoming rather than remote and approachable only through an intermediary. That intermediary was only permitted to approach the seat of God's power at certain times and then only after performing complex rituals. We no longer are constrained to only approach our Father in such a restrictive manner.

Steadfast: *Steadfast*, a word that has the meaning of permanence, determination and stability. It also has an underlying constancy of purpose. It is a character trait that is reassuring and builds confidence when you find it in another. It is one of the most frequently mentioned traits of our God. In Deuteronomy 32: 4, this description is recorded of God' character:

> "He is the Rock, his work is perfect: for all
> his ways are judgment: a God of truth and
> without iniquity, just and right is he."
> ~ Deuteronomy 32: 4

We have the example of this steadfastness in the promise that out of the house of David would come the Savior. Isaiah foretold of His attributes in Isaiah 16: 5.

> "In love a throne will be established; in
> faithfulness a man will sit on it one from

> the house of David one who in judging
> seeks justice and speeds the cause of
> righteousness."
> ~ Isaiah 16: 5

Honest: One who is *honest* is one who is genuine, free from deception, and his works are marked by integrity. Thus, would a God who instructs his people in honest dealings be anything less than honest in his dealings with them and yet still be deserving of honor, respect, and worship? I think not. Even when the honest replies to our queries are not what we wish to hear, we can and do get the true answers. He instructs us in what is honest and true. All throughout the teachings of the prophets and the law, we hear God's instruction on honest dealing. He promises, He will correct us when we do not live up to them.

In Psalms 23:3,4, we are told that He leads in the ways of righteousness, and the rod and staff are a comfort since they both protect and correct.

> "He guides me in paths of righteousness
> for his name's sake. Even though I walk
> through the valley of the shadow of death,
> I will fear no evil, for you are with me;
> your rod and your staff, they comfort me."
> ~ Psalms 23:3,4

Just: The word *just* means; one who conforms to fact and reason and one who that conforms to standards of correctness. It implies that the standards are published and comprehensible for all. All throughout His word we are given these standards that God uses to mete out His justice. Also, God has declared to us that position and status do not hold weight in his justice. He promises to deal equally with all people.

This is declared to us in both the Old and New Testaments. It is stated in many places that the Lord loves justice, and it will be used to measure and weigh our actions. Most reassuring is the statement that social standing, political pull, and depth of purse will have absolutely no influence on the justice dispensed. In dealing justly with us, He expects us to deal justly with one another.

In Psalms 11: 7 we are told;

> "For the Lord is righteous, he loves justice;
> the upright will see his face."

Again in Isaiah 28: 17, we are told;

> "I will make justice the measuring line and
> righteousness the plumb line; hail will
> sweep away your refuge, the lie, and water
> will overflow your hiding place."

Finally, in the New Testament book of Romans we are assured;

> "but glory, honor and peace for everyone
> who does good: first for the Jew, then for
> the Gentile. For God does not show
> favoritism. All who sin apart from the law
> will also perish apart from the law, and all
> who sin under the law will be judged by
> the law. For it is not those who hear the
> law who are righteous in God's sight, but it
> is those who obey the law who will be
> declared righteous."
> ~ Romans 2: 10-13

When we bring our failings, our troubles and triumphs to rest before him we have total confidence that they will be dealt with in absolute justice that, as promised, will be tempered by His grace and mercy.

Consistent: One of the most reassuring attributes of God is that he is consistent. For God to be *consistent*; means that He possesses of a firmness of purpose and has a coherence of message. With our limited understanding, sometimes it appears that contradictions occur, but as we gain understanding and knowledge, we come to see the consistency throughout. Consistency includes holding everyone to the same known standards so that there is no question about which standards apply to whom or when they are to be enforced. Consistency is found in the fact that the rules remain the same day to day, year to year, and age to age.

In Leviticus we are instructed:

> "You are to have the same law for the
> foreigner and the native-born. I am the
> Lord your God."
> ~ Leviticus 24: 22

As Hebrews 13: 8 tells us,

> "Jesus Christ is the same yesterday and
> today and forever."
> ~ Hebrews 13: 8

Thus, in summary, we can rest in the faith and confidence that the one who will be seated on the throne of judgment is the one who is true. He is one who is wholly just, steadfast, honest, and consistent. Also, He will be the one who has in merciful provision offered us the grace of surety for our forgiveness. This gives one a sense of solidity, stability, and security. So in great thanksgiving we look to commemorate the Advent of Our Lord and Savior.

> "I love you, Lord, my strength. The Lord is
> my rock, my fortress and my deliverer; my
> God is my rock, in whom I take refuge, my
> shield and the horn of my salvation, my
> stronghold. I called to the Lord, who is
> worthy of praise, and I have been saved
> from my enemies.
> ~ Psalms 18: 1-3

Later we are told,

> "And the God of all grace, who called you
> to his eternal glory in Christ, after you
> have suffered a little while, will himself
> restore you and make you strong, firm and
> steadfast."
> ~ 1 Peter 5: 10

On this steadfast, loving, and immutable rock we can build in confidence and faith. On this consistent loving kindness, we can rest with a sure knowledge that He is with us. On His bedrock honesty we can hold that our faith is true. On our trust in the perfect justice that is tempered with grace and mercy, we can rejoice. This rock gives us shelter from the storms, the burning sun and will conceal from those who would cause us harm.

The Wonder of Advent

Advent, is that wonderful anticipatory season where we look forward to celebrating the coming of Christ. Isn't it marvelous that God after so long deigned to again come in a form that we would be able to walk and talk with without special precautions. Consider the magnitude of the love that our God has shown for us that he sought us out where we were and is continuing to seek His children where ever they have wandered. In this act, He seeks only to persuade, not to coerce or force, our return to the joy of his companionship.

In Psalms 121:1, the question is asked:

> "I lift up my eyes to the mountains where
> does my help come from?"

With Advent we can answer that, our help came in the lowly form of an adorable baby laid in a manger. Yet again, God demonstrates to us that His ways are not ours, for we tend to look for our salvation to come in majesty and power not in humility and meekness. He came not in majestic power but in humble strength of the soul. Once again, we understand how thoroughly we should heed the warning given to us through King Solomon.

> "Trust in the Lord with all your heart and
> lean not on your own understanding; in all
> your ways submit to him, and he will make
> your paths straight."
> ~ Proverbs 3: 5, 6

Truly the one thing that always brings me up short every time, is the fact that He came, fully aware of the cost that He would be required to pay to satisfy our debt. He came knowing that He would have to suffer and die. Including the knowledge, that for a period during that act He would have to suffer the greatest pain ever; that of having the Father turn away from him. That pain is only shadowed in our understanding by the ache in our hearts that can only alleviated when we turn and commit to walking before God. The reason, Jesus accepted that a holy God would turn away from Him as He assumed the totality of the burden of our sins. This was the only thing that caused our Messiah to cry out in pain.

No longer do we need to ask to be shown the extent of God's love as the psalmist did in Psalms 17: 7 when he requested;

> "Show me the wonders of your great love,
> you who save by your right hand those
> who take refuge in you from their foes."

With the birth of Jesus our Savior, this wonder became flesh. Our refuge became knowable as He knows us intimately. Wonder is an emotion very closely aligned to worship and awe. God has given us such a great cause for astonishment or admiration that we can only marvel. Is there anything that excites more amazed admiration? It is an awesomely mysterious miracle that He considers us worthy of this sacrifice. Our rapt attention is a reasonable act of worship, for this love is certainly out of our normal experience.

> "Give praise to the Lord, proclaim his
> name; make known among the nations
> what he has done. Sing to him, sing praise
> to him; tell of all his wonderful acts. Glory
> in his holy name; let the hearts of those
> who seek the Lord rejoice. Look to the
> Lord and his strength; seek his face
> always."
> ~ 1 Chronicles 16: 8-11

How awesome is it that the God who spoke the universe into being considers one weak rebellious portion of creation to be worth the consideration and effort expressed in the love expressed in the Advent season? It is almost beyond comprehension that we are loved and yearned for to such a great extent. What expressions of joy and gratitude are due? Is it any wonder that we are struck with awe when we consider this love? Can we not join in with the rest of creation in celebration?

> "Rejoice with him, you heavens, and let all of God's angels worship him. Rejoice with his people, you nations, and let all the angels be strengthened in him. For he will avenge the blood of his servants; he will take revenge against his enemies. He will repay those who hate him and cleanse the land for his people."
> ~ Deuteronomy 32: 43 (NLT)

It is undoubtedly the most humbling and wonderful act. The one who spoke creation into being deigned to leave behind His glory and riches in heaven. He purposed to come down and take the journey to become our Savior and Kinsman Redeemer in acts of sacrificial forgiveness and love.

The Reason for the Advent

Yet I continue to be drawn to exploring the question, why. What were the reasons and purpose that necessitated God to going through the process that resulted in the Messiah coming to frail, faulty, failing mankind offering such a magnificent gift to ones so totally undeserving? This gift would require leaving behind the glories and joys of heaven, knowingly coming into contact with the literal filth that had entered creation, walking determinedly toward a voluntary separation from the Father, and facing the need to be forsaken all that was deeply loved and adored in order to offer a cleansing cure for mankind. Perhaps a clue can be found in the very first chapter of the first book of the Bible. We were made in his likeness and for a companionship union with the Godhead. For it is written:

> "Then God said, "Let us make mankind in
> our image, in our likeness, so that they
> may rule over the fish in the sea and the
> birds in the sky, over the livestock and all
> the wild animals, and over all the creatures
> that move along the ground."
> ~ Genesis 1: 26-27

Later in Genesis, we are given just an inkling of what that daily companionship might have been like. As it is implied that it was customary for God to walk and talk with Adam in the evening of each day. This is mentioned in the account that tells us of how man fell out of this intimate communion. This companionship can also be seen generally within the structure of the covenant of union given to man and woman at the beginning.

> "This is now bone of my bones and flesh
> of my flesh; she shall be called 'woman,'
> for she was taken out of man." That is why
> a man leaves his father and mother and is
> united to his wife, and they become one
> flesh. Adam and his wife were both naked,
> and they felt no shame."
> ~ Genesis 2: 23-25

Why was it that there was no shame? Could it have been because there was nothing to hide? Could it be that not one thing that was unknown, nothing held back but all was gladly shared and totally loved and entirely loving? So when shame (the feeling of the need to hold back from examination) entered in with sinning and God had to let us go our way bearing with the consequences of those actions, did that break a completeness that would require a mending and repair?

Timothy Keller in his book *King's Cross* likened the relationship that Christ left behind in heaven to a dance. In it he says,

> "The Father, the Son, and the Spirit are pouring love and joy and adoration into the other, each one serving the other. They are infinitely seeking one another's glory, and so God is infinitely seeking one another's glory, and so God is infinitely happy. And if it's true that this world has been created by this triune God, then ultimate reality is a dance."[6]

What if we were created to be a portion of this dance? For at the beginning, it is thought that God was wont to walk and talk with man in the cool of the evening (Genesis 3: 8). Then consider just what a hole we left behind when we decided to go our ways as each considered best in their own minds? Again, I come to the sense of completeness given in God's original language (Hebrew) to the number four.

So once we left the dance our partners would greatly desire our return. Now it becomes necessary that for us to be fit partners in this joyous dance once again, a repairing would be required to undo the damage done by sin. The road to this would require a three-step process only made possible by an overwhelmingly great love and the deep desire of a gracious and forgiving God. It required first the manumission of those enslaved to the things of the world. Then it required a means of complete reconciliation for the repentant to be able to again freely approach God without shame. Finally, it would give us guidance for our preparation for an anticipated glorious reunion with our Creator in a gloriously joyous, continual fellowship, intimate companionship, and mutual adoration with the Creator as we were made to be. All these could only be offered at the proper time in God's all-encompassing plan. For He has told us through the psalmist in Psalms 75 verses 1 and 2;

> We praise you, God, we praise you, for your Name is near; people tell of your wonderful deeds. You say, "I choose the appointed time; it is I who judge with equity.

This reconciliation, which has come to us, is rather pointedly summarized in the book of Romans, which points out that this reconciliation was made possible through the perfect life and sacrificial death of Jesus. The writer of the book; then points us to the restored relationship that is now available.

> "If we were reconciled to God through the death of his Son while we were still enemies, now that <u>we have been reconciled</u>, how much more certain is it that we will be saved by his life? And not only that: we even take pride in God through our Lord Jesus Christ, the one through whom we now have a <u>restored relationship</u> with God. So, in the same way that sin entered the world through one person, and death came through sin, so death spread to all human beings with the result that all sinned."
> ~ Romans 5: 10-12 (CEB)

In the end, I could not escape that this priceless child, whose advent is so joyously celebrated, intentionally came in this most unexpected manner in order to provide us the way of salvation which ultimately went through the cross.

Essay: Manumission

The first necessary step required for our being able to return to a right standing and relationship with God would be that we are free to choose and decide for ourselves, individually, that this relationship is something we desire and will treasure. Manumission comes to us from the Latin; it is the act of releasing from the hand; or the process of letting a bondservant or slave go free. [7] It is His desire that his companions come to him freely and of their own will. He showed us what would need to be done for us when He instituted two opportunities for man to deal with one another in a Godly manner. The first is the responsibility of the Guardian Redeemer. The second is the institution of a Year of Jubilee. These institutions were established under the Law which was given to inform us as to what needed to be perfectly performed daily in order to be qualified to independently return into original standing with God. By the institution of these standards of forgiveness God let us see that we would not be able to perfectly adhere to His Law of Righteousness. Both of these institutions would prefigure the purpose that necessitated the Advent of Christ. He would need to come as our Guardian Redeemer to stand our surety for the fulfillment of all of our debts and to restore our right standing within the family of God.

> "I, the Lord, have called you in righteousness; I will take hold of your hand. I will keep you and will make you to be a covenant for the people and a light for the Gentiles, to open eyes that are blind, to free captives from prison and to release from the dungeon those who sit in darkness. "I am the Lord; that is my name! I will not yield my glory to another or my praise to idols.
> ~ Isaiah 42: 6-8

The institution, purpose, description, and requirements of these rites for restoration and return to a right standing within the family can be found in the Old Testament book of Leviticus. This book describes the rights and responsibilities of the Guardian Redeemer. It, also, creates a means of forgiveness and restoration above and beyond that which is to be performed by the Guardian Redeemer. God instituted the form, frequency and requirements for the Year of Jubilee.

Guardian Redeemer: This responsibility was basically given to the head of the family or a descendant of the eldest son of the family to stand as Guardian Redeemer for the entire tribe (Leviticus 25: 25-55). It works back from the nearest living relative to the head of the clan, tribe or nation. The responsibilities include the following:

- The privilege and responsibility is given to the nearest living relative.
- Stand surety for the debts of the family members who have found themselves in difficulty.
- Redeem them if at all possible before the coming of the year of Jubilee
- Return them to a right standing within the family and tribe.

Year of Jubilee: As it was established, this year was to be incumbent upon the entire nation, and its celebration was to start on the Day of Atonement at the end of the seventh Sabbatical year. This celebration was to continue throughout the fiftieth year [Leviticus 25: 7-24]. This year is a culmination of the time set asides for the commemoration of God's love, provision, and discipline (starting with the Sabbath on the seventh day; Atonement given during the seventh month; Sabbatical year where the land rested in the seventh year; after seven Sabbatical years during the seventh month came the commencement of the Year of Jubilee). It was to be an example to the world of the grace and justice that God would bring to the world. The fundamentals of celebrating this year include the following:

- A return to your birthright land and family
- A year of rest where God will fulfill all needs.
- A year of liberation from enslavement.

- All that is released during the Jubilee will be dedicated as holy to the Lord.

Now in Christ, we have in one all that was prefigured by these two institutions. Christ is our guardian. Throughout scripture God is shown as guarding his people jealously and zealously. Most frequently, the Lord is shown as a Shepherd as in,

> "The LORD is my Shepherd"
> ~ Psalm 23: 1

God has continually redeemed people out all sorts of sticky situations that they had gotten themselves into on innumerable occasions. The evidence that He desires the freedom of His people can be found in the many times He has brought His people out of bondage and exile, returning them to the land that He had given them when He had first called them out to bring light to the world with His covenant with Abraham.

> "I have swept away your offenses like a cloud, your sins like the morning mist. Return to me, for I have redeemed you."
> Sing for joy, you heavens, for the Lord has done this; shout aloud, you earth beneath.
> Burst into song, you mountains, you forests and all your trees, for the Lord has redeemed Jacob, he displays his glory in Israel."
> ~ Isaiah 44:22, 23

In Christ we have the ultimate offering of redemption. In the New Testament book of Colossians, this gracious gift of redemption is confirmed to all of us.

> "and giving joyful thanks to the Father, who has qualified you to share in the inheritance of his holy people in the kingdom of light. For he has rescued us from the dominion of darkness and brought us into the kingdom of the Son he loves, in whom we have redemption, the forgiveness of sins."
> ~ Colossians 1: 12-14

By His making the only payment that would be sufficient for our transgressions and being willing make the perfect sacrifice for needed for our redemption, he then graciously offered us the opportunity to choose to be his holy people who are dedicated to God. He has provided us just cause for great jubilation. In the Old Testament, God says of those people called to him that they are to be a holy people. This was not just those called to be of the priesthood, but all people. As it says in the psalms,

> I say of the holy people who are in the land, "They are the noble ones in whom is all my delight."
> ~ Psalm 16: 3

Then we find it said in the New Testament:

> "But you are a chosen people, a royal priesthood, a holy nation, God's special possession, that you may declare the praises of him who called you out of darkness into his wonderful light. Once you were not a people, but now you are the people of God; once you had not received mercy, but now you have received mercy."
> ~ 1 Peter 2: 9, 10

So with Advent, Christ, our Guardian Redeemer, came to the world to begin the process of fulfilling the requirements for being the sufficiency of atonement and payment to redeem us from slavery to sin by perfectly fulfilling the Law. He also came to guide us toward the jubilation of our restoration to man's right standing with God. Then as ones who have been restored during a year of Jubilee, those who accept are dedicated as holy to the Lord.

> "The death he died, he died to sin once for all; but the life he lives, he lives to God. In the same way, count yourselves dead to sin but alive to God in Christ Jesus."
> ~ Romans 6: 10, 11

Essay: Reconciliation

The definition of reconciliation is; "to cause people or groups to become friendly again after an argument or disagreement."[8] To this I would add to bring together again after causing grievance or harm. In this instance much of the movement toward reconciliation is made by the aggrieved party. As we have caused great grievance to God, it was His decision to offer a plan to reconcile. Advent is the beginning of the final chapter of the story of His plan for our being welcomed back into His intimate companionship.

This eternal plan that God set in motion with Advent, demonstrates His sacrificial love for his creation. It is an overwhelming example of His capacity for sacrificial forgiveness. This culminates in His offering in our stead the sacrificial atonement for our imperfections which covered the payment that it would always be impossible for us to ever be able to offer sufficiently in restitution.

These are defined as:

1. **Sacrificial Love:** This is a love that willingly gives up thought of self for the needs of the loved one. This is not one that thinks of benefit to self but of the building up of the object of its affection. Good parents are an earthly picture of this love, and in extreme example, parents have laid down their lives so that their child might prosper.

2. **Sacrificial Forgiveness:** Forgiveness in its truest form demands a sacrifice on the part of the forgiver in that it releases the offender from a need to make restitution or from fear of retribution. In the extreme the one giving forgiveness absorbs the entire cost of the offenses.

3. **Sacrificial Atonement:** Atonement is the reparation for an offense or injury. Sacrificial atonement is making reparations for offenses committed by another. In the case of Christ, He paid the reparations

for each and every one of us before our supremely just God.

In the Bible's book of Hosea, God had one of his prophets demonstrate, in human terms, what the cost of His plan would look like. To me, this book was one of the more baffling books of the Bible in that God has one of his chosen prophets act in ways that most men would not or could not bring themselves to perform. In it He has his prophet take a woman most would never have considered worthy as a wife. Then He would have him forgive and forgive again her straying from their marriage. Taking take her back every time she strayed, even to the point of paying for her freedom from those to whom she had given control over her life!

1. <u>Sacrificial Love</u>:

In Hosea we are given an example of this type of love. In that instance God would tell his chosen prophet to go and select a wife from among women who were impure. In this God shows us on a human level the breadth of his desire for us. It depicts God's love for a humanity that is constantly chasing after impure and ungodly things.

> When the Lord began to speak through Hosea, the Lord said to him, "Go, marry a promiscuous woman and have children with her, for like an adulterous wife this land is guilty of unfaithfulness to the Lord."
> ~ Hosea 1: 2

I, then remembered, how times the names of those chosen to carry God's instruction to humanity could carry a message as well. So I looked at the meaning given to the name, Hosea son of Beeri [ben-Beeri]. What I found was Hosea is a form of Joshua so it carries a meaning of salvation. The surname ben-Beeri was a bit more difficult to determine. It is thought in several places to signify a well or water source. So it could imply life sustaining water. In the New Testament book of John, Jesus refers to himself as the "living water".

> 'Jesus answered her, "If you knew the gift of God and who it is that asks you for a drink, you would have asked him and he would have given you living water." "Sir," the woman said, "you have nothing to draw with and the well is deep. Where can you get this living water? Are you greater than our father Jacob, who gave us the well and drank from it himself, as did also his sons and his livestock?" Jesus answered, "Everyone who drinks this water will be thirsty again, but whoever drinks the water I give them will never thirst. Indeed, the water I give them will become in them a spring of water welling up to eternal life."
> ~ John 4: 10-14

2. <u>Sacrificial Forgiveness</u>:

In many ways this can be seen as a very great act of mercy and a foregoing of exacting the just consequences of the actions taken by another. In the case of Hosea this comes at least twice. The first occurrence is when he forgives the adulteries committed by his soon to be wife prior to entering into marriage. The second time occurs, after she leaves the marriage to continue after these activities. He does not forsake his wife who has left his home and committed many acts of adultery. At the behest of God, Hosea receives her back. By the law, he would have been well within it to have put her away by divorce. Yet he takes her back into his house. God, in Hosea 2 shows what the just consequences of these adulterous pursuits would be by likening what the northern kingdom of Israel was doing to an adulterous mother.

> "Rebuke your mother, rebuke her, for she is not my wife, and I am not her husband. Let her remove the adulterous look from her face and the unfaithfulness from between her breasts. Otherwise I will strip her naked and make her as bare as on the day she was born; I will make her like a desert, turn her into a parched land, and slay her with thirst. I will not show my

> love to her children, because they are the
> children of adultery. Their mother has been
> unfaithful and has conceived them in
> disgrace.
> ~ Hosea 2: 2-5

Yet in the very next chapter, He asks Hosea to go and demonstrate remarkable mercy and forgiveness.

> The Lord said to me, "Go, show your love
> to your wife again, though she is loved by
> another man and is an adulteress. Love her
> as the Lord loves the Israelites, though
> they turn to other gods and love the sacred
> raisin cakes."
> ~ Hosea 3: 1

In this compare and contrast, God shows us just how great is His desire to forgive and forget our transgressions. On one hand we are reminded of the just consequences for our adulterous acts (chapter two) then showing us the extent to which He would forgive by having His prophet Hosea demonstrate great forgiveness (chapter 3) out of an immense love. A great love that goes over and above what most natural men would be capable of achieving. Jesus expressed this yearning to forgive and accept back in his sorrow over Jerusalem.

> "Jerusalem, Jerusalem, you who kill the
> prophets and stone those sent to you, how
> often I have longed to gather your children
> together, as a hen gathers her chicks under
> her wings, and you were not willing. Look,
> your house is left to you desolate. I tell
> you, you will not see me again until you
> say, 'Blessed is he who comes in the name
> of the Lord.'"
> ~ Luke 13: 34, 35

3. <u>Sacrificial Atonement</u>:

Many of us could not make adequate reparation and restitution for the debt of harm or injury that we've done to one another, let alone be able to perfectly satisfy the debt we've incurred to God. In the book of Hosea, God has him not only go and seek out his wandering wife, but then He has him buy back her freedom from the ones holding her in slavery to adulterous actions. In the same way, after living perfectly according to the Laws of righteousness Jesus made himself the totally sufficient price to purchase our freedom from slavery to sin and make restitution for the harm we have caused.

Under the Laws of righteousness, the atoning sacrifice for life could only be made in blood. In addition, the sacrificial offering had to be the most perfect specimen; if it was not it would not be sufficient to make the atonement.

> "I will set my face against any Israelite or any foreigner residing among them who eats blood, and I will cut them off from the people. For the life of a creature is in the blood, and I have given it to you to make atonement for yourselves on the altar; it is the blood that makes atonement for one's life. Therefore I say to the Israelites, "None of you may eat blood, nor may any foreigner residing among you eat blood."
> ~ Leviticus 17: 10-12

There were other restitutions specified, but the greatest possible offering for the most complete covering of sin was in a blood sacrifice.

In Hosea's case God had him sacrifice his pride, dignity and treasure in order to obtain the release and return of his wife with the price thought to be the price of a female slave.

> "So I bought her for fifteen shekels [9] of silver and about a homer and a lethek [10] of barley."
> ~ Hosea 3: 3

Jesus would also do this for all of humanity, so great was God's love and desire to have us back in union with Him. He, Jesus, did not stand on His dignity and pride, he associated with those most in need of healing. His treasures and comforts were left behind when He came to walk with us on earth. Then after living life in perfect righteousness, He offered Himself as the payment for all of us. The writer of Romans put it thusly:

> "This righteousness is given through the faithfulness of Jesus Christ to all who believe. There is no difference between Jew and Gentile, for all have sinned and fall short of the glory of God, and all are justified freely by his grace through the redemption that came by Christ Jesus. God presented Christ as a sacrifice of atonement, through the shedding of his blood - - to be received by faith. He did this to demonstrate his righteousness, because in his forbearance he had left the sins committed beforehand unpunished - - he did it to demonstrate his righteousness at the present time, so as to be just and the one who justifies those who have faith in Jesus."
> ~ Romans 3: 22-26

In the Book of Hosea, God has given us a picture of what it would take for Him to achieve our reconciliation. It is for us to take the next step because by His Love, His Forgiveness, and His Sacrificial Atonement, He has paid the price needed for our return. He then let us know that there would be a period between the substitution sacrifice that was necessary for the propitiation for all of every one of our transgressions and the restoration of the total intimate companionship relationship.

> "For the Israelites will live many days without king or prince, without sacrifice or sacred stones, without ephod or household gods. Afterward the Israelites will return and seek the Lord their God and David their king. They will come trembling to the Lord and to his blessings in the last days."
> ~ Hosea 3: 4, 5

This might be thought of as a description of the time many refer to as the "Church Age". It tells of a time when Israel will again be cut off from Temple worship for a period in preparation for the complete restoration.

Essay: Restoration:

With the Advent of Christ, God has, in His time, set in place all the elements necessary for the restoration of man to his right standing within Creation. The Law has been fulfilled, totally and perfectly, in the life lived by our Messiah, Jesus of Nazareth. His willing sacrifice for us made the only sufficient Atonement possible. It is now for each of us to decide accept the gift, which then requires the believer to work toward the day when our full restoration will occur. In essence this period could be likened to the traditional period of betrothal, where both the bride and the groom work independently preparing for the expected time of completing their union. Christ, our betrothed husband has told us what He will be accomplishing during our time of betrothal.

> "My Father's house has many rooms; if that were not so, would I have told you that I am going there to prepare a place for you? And if I go and prepare a place for you, I will come back and take you to be with me that you also may be where I am. You know the way to the place where I am going."
> ~ John 14: 2-4

The groom has told us that he has gone ahead to prepare suitable places for us. So what is that which we are working to prepare ourselves for? When many of us say "marriage", we picture the purpose of procreation. Actually, the covenant marriage is meant to be so much more than that. It is meant to be a union that is jubilantly total and completely joyous. As such, it is this union that is so eagerly anticipated, expected, prepared for diligently, will be utterly transforming. God has remained constant, faithful, forgiving, and true throughout the innumerable stumblings and false starts of the beloved, even to the point of leaving behind the glorious home in heaven to ensure that the beloved would be free to come to Him when the time of waiting would be completed.

Our part in the preparation has been summed up in what has been called the "Great Commission." What we are asked to do is remarkably simple: we are to share the "Good News" of our salvation, we are to share our expectant joy and invite others to accept God's gift and then join us in preparing for the coming reunion.

> "Then the eleven disciples went to Galilee, to the mountain where Jesus had told them to go. When they saw him, they worshiped him; but some doubted. Then Jesus came to them and said, "All authority in heaven and on earth has been given to me. Therefore go and make disciples of all nations, baptizing them in the name of the Father and of the Son and of the Holy Spirit, and teaching them to obey everything I have commanded you. And surely I am with you always, to the very end of the age."
> ~ Matthew 28: 16-20

As each party prepares for a resumption of the dance that was broken in Eden by sinning, we can anticipate a glorious celebration with its resumption at the End of Time. This dance is intricate and intimate, yet simple and satisfying, founded in the assurance of the complete wisdom and justice of the leader in this dance. It is the give and take of knowing the other completely and being known totally by your partner. It is the weaving of a companionship that always rests in the confidence of there being one who wants just to be there with you and for you. It is this companionship that desires and rejoices in serving the other. It has a depth of communication that results in the union moving and acting as one. Above all it is rooted in the admiration and adoration of the other. It is evidenced in the readiness and joy in the delighted serving of each other. This is what we lost in Eden and what we are looking forward to when the complete restoration will be accomplished. For since Eden and made possible by the Advent of Christ, God has looked forward to (and His people have yearned to hear) the joyous shout:

The Seasons of Advent

"Hallelujah!
For our Lord God Almighty reigns
Let us rejoice and be glad and give him
glory! For the wedding of the Lamb has
come, and his bride has made herself ready.
Fine linen, bright and clean, was given her
to wear."
~ Revelation 19: 6, 7, & 8

Footnotes:

pg. 33   [1] Expansion of the given names found in Ezra 10:2

Shechaniah = God has taken up His abode,

Jehiel = carried away by God

Elam = Hidden, Hidden Time, Eternity, Young Man or Always.

Ezra = Help, with the connotation of Strong Vision.

Eloheinu (OJT) [Our God] = Lord

am ha'aretz women (OJT) [strange wives] = ignorant women

Israel = God strives

pg. 37   [2] Merriam Webster online dictionary: definition providence

pg. 45   verses referenced:

[3] "Enoch walked faithfully with God; then he was no more, because God took him away."

~ Genesis 5:24

[4] "Cain said to the LORD, "My punishment is more than I can bear. Today you are driving me from the land, and I will be hidden from your presence; I will be a restless wanderer on the earth, and whoever finds me will kill me." But the LORD said to him, "Not so; if anyone kills Cain, he will suffer vengeance seven times over. Then the LORD put a mark on Cain so that no one who found him would kill him."

~ Genesis 4: 13-15

[5] "With the coming of dawn, the angels urged Lot, saying, "Hurry! Take your wife and your two daughters who are here, or you will be swept away when the city is punished." When he hesitated, the men grasped his hand and the hands of his wife and of his two daughters and led them safely out of the city, for the Lord was merciful to them."

~ Genesis 19: 15, 16

pg. 60 [6] Timothy Keller, *King's Cross* (Penguin Books, Dutton, USA, 2011);7

pg. 62 [7] Online Etymology Dictionary: Manumission

pg. 66 [8] Merriam Webster online Dictionary: definition reconciliation

pg. 70 conversions: [9] shekel about 170 g. of silver

[10] lethek thought to be about 195 kg. of barley

Unless notated all Biblical quotations are from the New International Translation

Other translations used: ASV (American Standard Version)

CEB (Common English Bible)

EXB (EXpanded Bible)

KJV (King James Version)

NLT (New Living Translation)

OJT (Orthodox Jewish Translation)